Off the Mat

Off the Mat

Building Winners in Life

by
JOHN E. DU PONT

Head Wrestling Coach, Villanova University
and Founder of *Team Foxcatcher*

JAMESON BOOKS
Ottawa, Illinois

Jameson books are available at special discount for bulk purchases
for sales promotions, premiums, fund-raising, or educational use.
Special editions of book excerpts can also be created to specification.

For information and catalog requests contact:

Jameson Books, Inc.
P.O. Box 738
Ottawa, IL 61350
(815) 434-7905

10   9   8   7   6   5   4   3   2

Printed in the United States of America

ISBN: 0-915463-54-7

Second Printing 2005

To my beloved father,
WILLIAM DU PONT, JR.,
a great citizen, patriot, and winner,
to whom I owe my life.

Contents

Introduction

I LOVE athletics. I love people. And I love America. Simple statements, but nonetheless true and complete.

For some time I have been keenly aware of the need for the athletes of America, both the young and the not-so-young, to be model citizens. Athletes today are the role models for our citizens of tomorrow. Whether it be at the Little League level or at the highest levels of professional sports, in large measure our athletes set the stage for the conduct of America and her people. It is to sports and athletes that America looks for the example.

Tragically, in recent years the number of athletes who have so unfortunately become involved in drug abuse and other improper conduct has increased dramatically, and those misdeeds have been widely publicized by the news media. With that has come a misleading and criminal message of confusion and conflict to the youth of America from those we have long held as our heroes and our role models.

These athletes have quite simply given America the wrong example.

I believe with all my heart that citizenship is a blessing, not a right, and that good citizenship is a duty, not an option. It is to each of us a public trust, a sacred trust. And athletes at all levels have a special duty to be examples of that quality citizenship to all who may see. It is my belief, indeed my dream, that all athletes can and will be examples of positive citizenship for all the world to follow proudly.

As a young boy I learned from the example of my father, William du Pont, a truly great American patriot and pioneer, what it takes to win and what it takes to be an honorable American citizen. As a competitive athlete for many years, I learned through experience what it takes to win. And today, as a coach of over six hundred young people in our Villanova and *Team Foxcatcher* programs, I understand from another challenging perspective what it takes to win. On—and off—the mat.

Our challenge as coaches and leaders of athletes everywhere, indeed our obligation and responsibility, is first and foremost to build winners in life, to build men and women who will be prepared for life and who will understand and exemplify the character traits of good citizenship on—and off—the field of competition.

My hope is that through my humble efforts I can in some way help our talented American athletes and their selflessly dedicated coaches more fully to understand what it takes to be a winner in life and the importance of good citizenship by our athletes to the American destiny of greatness.

John Eleutheré du Pont
Villanova, Pennsylvania

Chapter I

Why Americans Love Sports

A MERICANS love a winner. Whether in sports, politics, business or fiction, Americans love a winner. Names like Namath, Roosevelt and the fictional Rocky Balboa are household treasures not just because they won on the field of play, but equally important because they won off the field. Or as we say in wrestling, "off the mat."

Joe Namath had bad knees and a football league that Vince Lombardi (just two years before) intimated shouldn't even be playing against a National Football League champion. And everyone knew that any NFL team could beat any AFL team any day of the week on any field. Everyone but Joe Namath and the Jets, that is. The Jets won Super Bowl III against Kansas City, and America loved Broadway Joe.

On a cold March day in 1933, a crippled Franklin Delano Roosevelt assumed the Presidency after the greatest financial collapse that then had ever been experienced in our country. He took on a crippled America heading for the bottom of a Great Depression and a Second World War. America doubted itself. He offered us a "New Deal," and he challenged us to understand that "We have nothing to fear, but fear itself." America rallied, fought, worked and dreamed. And in the process she became the greatest economic and military power on earth.

I tried to console myself on October 20, 1987, as I drove from my home that crisp autumn morning to our training facility for early morning practice on the wrestling mat with my student athletes. I remembered that America had recovered from the Great Depression and the stock market crash of 1929. In the coolness of that early October morning I needed to remember that lesson very much, because on the previous day in the great 500 point crash on Wall Street. But my place that day, as every day, was to be on the mat and in the pool with the student athletes. The financial matters would be resolved, and the resources necessary for John du Pont to carry on *Team Foxcatcher* and other of our programs would be regrouped and restored. Our national will to win and the strength of America would prevail.

The fictional champion Rocky Balboa represents the true archetypical American hero. Against all odds, with unrecognized talent and unparalleled determination, he became the boxing champion of the world. His is the American story told in dramatic form: a nation of immigrants with little education, who form the core of a great people. In the words of Emma Lazarus' poem engraved on the base of the Statue of Liberty, we are the "tired (and) poor ... the huddled masses yearning to breathe free." I know. Six generations ago, my family came to these shores, worked hard to realize the blessings our nation offered, prospered, and are today living out the meaning of the American Dream.

Some have agreed with Lazarus' implicit characterization that America is a nation made up of everybody else's losers, "the wretched refuse of their teeming shores." I do not. Our forefathers created a nation made up of those who saw beyond the horizon, who dared to dream of adventure, and who risked ultimate failure for the opportunity to achieve ultimate success for themselves and for their posterity. Generations of immigrants were not losers; rather they were and they are today in large measure the winners, the dreams, the builders. My ancestor E. I. du Pont de Nemours built the chemical company that bears his name today.

America has been a nation of Rockys since its inception. Two hundred years ago, who would have bet on George Washington and his ragtag army of farmers? Not even Congress was willing to give much beyond moral support, and at that time there were more deserters than fighters. To be sure, there were few real soldiers. But at Valley Forge, in the depths of adversity, an American Army was born and forged into tempered steel by the refiner's fire of that hellishly miserable winter of 1777–78.

Today as I walk those same fields of Valley Forge near the home where I was reared and where I now live, I still marvel at the strength of Washington's moral leadership and the capacity he had for eliciting the highest levels of dedication and performance in his soldiers. As a coach I build winners by making the athletes first believe in themselves and only then by building their skill. In think maybe that's what George Washington did. And there have been days when I certainly would have liked to have asked him how.

People don't realize the serious and dire straits that George Washington and this young nation faced during that 1777 winter. Washington's army almost starved to death. I don't know what they are teaching kids in school these days, but it surely isn't about the struggles that gave birth to this nation and the freedoms we all enjoy today. That determination, courage, resolve and will to win that Washington's army demonstrated in Valley Forge is precisely what America needs today.

I have the desire not only to be a winner myself, but also to help other people become winners. I brought the youthful wrestling team from Puerto Rico to Valley Forge for just that reason.

These student athletes from Puerto Rico were enormously impressed by the Valley Forge experience. I don't believe in ghosts and other elements of what is popularly called "mysticism" today, but I will tell anybody that there is a spirit that permeates Valley Forge that must have been left there by George Washington. Into Valley Forge went farmers and shopkeepers, and out came an army and a nation. And from that army came the will to win over the greatest armed force then on earth. Nothing could stop it. That is the American spirit we have inherited.

Good News

Americans love champions because we are optimists. We believe that tomorrow will be better than today. Each generation polled by the Gallup organization believes that the

America their children will inherit will be better than the one they themselves inherited from their parents. We believe, with Annie, that "The sun'll come out, tomorrow."

I believe that President Ronald Reagan's greatest strength and appeal is not his ideology, it is his unbounded and contagious optimism. He knows there is no "malaise" in the American spirit. He is confident that he can help create a better, stronger America. He believes in America and in her people. And Americans want to believe him.

Ironically, the news media generally does not share the President's sense of optimism. The only place in our newspapers or nightly television news broadcasts where there is good news is on the sports page. The front page, national and international news, state and local news are all filled with bad news: war, murder, good people gone bad, starvation, earthquakes, AIDS, crime, disasters, and, yes, role model athletes involved in drugs.

News is not just the retelling of current events. It is drama: whether it is television drama or print drama, it is drama. It is the telling of current events in dramatic fashion. And news drama is about tragedies.

Equally, because it depends on advertisers to pay the tab, it must raise anger, lust, fear or some other high emotion in order to "lock in" the viewer or reader to the program. Consider the success of such programs as the soap operas, *Sixty Minutes*, and others. People don't watch Tom Brokaw, Peter Jennings or Dan Rather to see how many airline passengers arrived safely at their destination, how many countries are at peace, how many Members of Congress are not going to be indicted or even what countries had beautiful, clear weather. There simply is no drama there.

I was living in California during the Vietnam era and saw a

7

story on the evening news one night that shocked me. I had just turned on the news when on came a story about how many UCLA students did not attend a protest rally on campus that day and what they did instead. It was like a new world opening up. Instead of looking at hundreds of students at the protest, viewers saw thousands of students who were dutifully attending their classes, doing experiments in the labs, or listening to a guest lecturer. We saw the 95 percent who did not protest. That was unique, but only worth one story because good news is not news. It is just a current event. So we join with singer Anne Murray whose voice like the crystal clear waters of her native Nova Scotia laments, "We sure could use a little good news today." And so we turn to the sports page.

Only the sports page is filled with good news about people we admire doing things we admire: the Masters' champion, the Heisman Trophy winner, the Cy Young Award, Olympic champions, the America's Cup, the World Series and the Super Bowl. Each represents something about us as a people that we want to believe in both as a nation and as individuals.

The sports pages tell of heroes. And anyone who has read the Greek tragedies knows that heroes do not have to be perfect to be heroes. In fact their very vulnerabilities make them more heroic, not less so. It is the pitcher who comes back after a devastating injury, the golfer who hasn't won since May but who comes from behind on the last day this week to win, the runner who finishes two hours behind everyone else in the marathon but finishes with pride, whom we cheer.

In politics, generally speaking, only those who get the most votes are remembered. In sports, our heroes are those who triumph over adversity regardless of the score. Glenn Cunningham is remembered as an Olympic champion; more important, he is remembered as the boy whose body was critically damaged in a fire, but in whose heart the fire of competition was stronger . . . strong enough to overcome the weakness of the body and win an Olympic gold medal.

The sports page covers them all. And the triumph and tragedy all make the athlete our real life dream in living color on CBS, NBC and ABC.

Only the Talented Need Apply

Athletic excellence is also a great class equalizer. Although there really are no economic class distinctions in America comparable to the classes of European nations, the resentments of our European ancestors remain strong in the United States.

We still strongly resent anyone who gets ahead because of "who they know, not what they know." We do not like influence peddling, nepotism or backroom deals. We are suspicious of anyone who succeeds on someone else's merits. I know all about this first hand. As a member of a prominent American family with wealth, all my life I have tried to demonstrate—probably because I had to—that I could achieve and win on my own as though my last name weren't du Pont. And I have met a lot of resentment and disbelief along the way. While some of it was very pointed and really quite painful, I learned as a young man to shrug it off because it said nothing about me but said everything

9

about my detractors. I learned to appreciate the value of hard work and desire.

Life, I believe, should be like athletic competition: 1) fair competition, 2) on an equal field of battle, 3) between contestants who got there through talent and determination alone. When those conditions are met, we accept the verdict. In reality, of course, life is not always like that. Perhaps that explains why so many rage against life's verdicts.

In America we are so concerned about the issue of fairness that in most sports we even allow "walk-ons" (people who are not discovered in traditional ways, i.e. through college recruiters, scouts, etc.) as a way of ensuring that each individual athlete receives a full and impartial tryout. But only the talented need apply. There is no other measure of success. With the world watching, the athlete either has it or he or she does not.

My sport of wrestling is a good example of what I am talking about. Our athletes can train in the best facilities in the world (we think we have that) under the direction of the best coaches. They can be pampered, peppered with PMA (positive mental attitude) or pushed to their limits in preparation. But once the wrestler is on the mat, he's alone. Whether he wins or loses is up to him. Not to his parents. Not to his team. Not to his coach. Just to him. Failure to grasp that essential fact costs more falls than probably any other single element in wrestling, particularly at the championship level. One of my wrestlers has twice lost the world championships because he hasn't yet shaken a subconscious self-doubt and realized that he is the only stumbling block between himself and that championship. Call it fear, call it negative attitude, whatever you like. The fact is that the last all-important ten percent of any effort is about 90 percent mental and 10 percent physical. In sports as nowhere else the rules of competition make talent and determination the only criteria for success.

Spectators

Another thing we love about sports is that we can all be a part of the game. In many ways, athletic competition is as much about the spectators as it is about the competitors. The fans are just as excited about the victory as are the athletes. And they cry just as sorrowfully as does the athlete when he or she loses.

Most athletic events (from wrestling to baseball) are staged events where every part of the field of play is judged by its relationship with the viewing audience. This is even more intense today when many sports are televised, and the audience outside the arena is many times larger than the audience inside. In many cases the rules are even changed to accommodate the needs of this new television audience (such as time outs for station breaks and advertisements). Perhaps it all began with David and Goliath where two people were chosen to represent everyone on the field of battle. However it started, this feeling that the athletes on the mat represent everyone present is very strong.

In this sense there are no spectators. Each person is participating physically or emotionally in the play of the game. The athletes do things physically that we all wish we could do. This is vicarious fulfillment. We live our dream through them. When the runner sprints, the wrestler pins or the pitcher sends a curve ball, we are doing it too. (If you don't believe that the spectators feel they are being represented on the field, just ask any football fan who has just seen his team make a major error what play should have been run and you'll see a real armchair strategist at work.)

This is all a fulfillment of one's self and self-image. What American boy hasn't dreamed that he is Joe Montana? What American girl hasn't dreamed she is Mary Lou Retton? And many of these "boys and girls" are considerably older than 21 years.

Competitive Spirit

Americans are competitive by nature, and I love it. It has been said that ours is a people with diverse national cultural backgrounds, proving the Darwinian theory of the survival of the fittest. While this ignores the strong sense of social conscience that underlies our national character, it is a good description of who came to America to begin with and what they taught us (generations of their children) about economic and social competition.

In my own family, competition was a part of my earliest memory. My mother, blessed with an indomitable spirit and zest for life, has won more than 33,000 trophies, ribbons and medals in equestrian events. And at age 90, she's not through yet!

Freedom is competition. We prize our freedom. We fight

for preservation of rights that others wouldn't dream of seeing in their lifetimes. We compete for the right to continue our lives as we see fit, not as the government does. This is what distinguishes our country from the nations of the world that live under the tyranny of Communism or other totalitarian systems. We demand "life, liberty, and the pursuit of happiness." This pursuit is a competitive one. We accept that, count on it, and determine to succeed through it.

Solidarity could never have been outlawed in America. We simply wouldn't stand for it. We'd either laugh at the attempt to muzzle the aspirations of millions of our fellow citizens, or throw the government out in a rage. The great strides forward made by the civil rights movement of the 1950's and '60's prove that. That's our competitive spirit. It changes our opinions of nations ("ping pong diplomacy" and China) and endears us to opponents (Nadia Komeneche). It recreates our world.

When I started the modern triathlon in 1966 there were only six people who entered the sport. Today more than one and a quarter million people compete in it annually. Such is the spirit of competition in America.

Bonding

Athletic events bond us together. They give a sense of community in a fast-changing, transient world. More than twenty percent of Americans move every five years. Wherever they move to, there are teams, schools and community sports to integrate them, to give them friends and to add joy and fulfillment to their lives.

It is interesting to watch how quickly the Milwaukee businessman who moves to Los Angeles changes from a Bucks fan to a Lakers fan. It is his sense of community and the Lakers are his bonding agent.

These events also bond families and friends. We all love movies, but we can't talk with each other in the theatre. At sporting events we are expected to talk with each other, laugh together, yell together and cry together. These events provide emotional interaction. At lunch, during breaks and around the table at dinner, sports offer the American family and our friends things to talk about, strategize about and wager on. It is more than idle chatter. It is bonding.

People identify with various teams as their own. It's not just that they follow a team's performance; they view themselves as part of the team. "I'm a Yankees fan" tells more about the fan than it does the team. It provides a statement of common linkage to others who may have nothing else in common. It cuts across racial divisions, religious differences and political alignments. And that's enough to bring together the true Yankees fans.

The True Believer

In 1951, the late Eric Hoffer, a longshoreman and a genius on understanding the nature of mass movements, wrote a little book entitled *The True Believer*.

The thesis of the book is that the true believer is a hitchhiker in life looking for an "ism" to catch a ride with. It is more important to find an "ism" to believe in than the specifics of which "ism." The converted are the easiest converts.

Now that war is no longer a prized national policy in Western democracies, now that education has weakened the hold of blind loyalty to governments and now that mass transportation and American mobility have weakened our distrust of people who are different from ourselves, mass movements have lost their appeal. But the basic need in people that was met by participating in mass movements is still present. There is still the intense need for belonging, heightened by the sense of alienation caused by industrial and post-industrial work systems and sharpened by the need to feel a sense of fulfillment outside one's own daily life.

Life for most people is routine. They are part of very little creative activity or of enthusiastic causes. They do things each day that look just like the things they did the day before. This often robs them of feelings of excellence, progress, or meaning. At some point many are prone to echo the old Peggy Lee song, "Is that all there is?" Religious or service activity fills that void for many. But for many others, sports is the only mechanism they have found to fill that place in their hearts.

Completion

Sports also speaks to another major psychological need that goes unfulfilled in modern society: a sense of completion. There are very few professions today that offer a sense of completion. In an economy that is growing even more service oriented, there is little opportunity to complete a project. Work must be done over, research is unending, and specialization prevents any one person from seeing the end product. And the individual always knows that it could have been done better, faster and more thoroughly. So even when the work stops, there is generally no emotional release.

That's what I like about wrestling. Despite the months and years of practice, there are always results. There's only one winner in a wrestling match. The decision is there for all to see, either to take pride in or to serve as an object lesson, and as an incentive for improvement the next time. The winner has won, the loser has lost. It is finished, both physically and psychologically. The athletes, coaches, teams and fans have to adjust to this changed circumstance. But win or lose, there is a sense of completion. And that is healthy for us all.

Role Model

Finally, athletes young and old provide a role model for modern society in today's fast-paced world where leaders of nations change as fast as the changing of the seasons. Kids look up to them. Young people idolize them. They are champions to young adults. And they provide fond memories for the aging.

That is why the spectacle of athletes using and selling drugs is so despicable. Particularly for the highly paid professional athletes, this is the most gross abdication of their inherent responsibility as public role models. While the circumstances that lead an athlete, professional or amateur, to use drugs vary enormously, and while each life destroyed by drug use is a human tragedy, I believe very strongly that the damage done to America as a whole by athletes who fail in their public responsibility is far greater. This is a national tragedy.

Theirs and ours is a great responsibility. We must be what America believes about itself: honest, determined, hardworking, fair and competitive. We must be magnanimous in victory, gracious in defeat. But most of all we must be good people, good athletes and good citizens.

That is what this book is all about. How do we distill, refine and apply the lessons of sports so that we may shoulder the burden of responsibility for being good, active citizens as the world faces the dawn of a new century? It will be a century of America's greatness if we make it so. It will be a century of America's decline if we permit it to be so.

Chapter II

Television and Sports

T ELEVISION has changed sports forever. Its impact is being extended into every level of sports competition from amateur college sports and the Olympics to every professional sport in America. There are even special television networks devoted exclusively to sports entertainment, and sports figures are lumped together in the news right beside entertainers, folk heroes and movie stars, to be followed by the *National Enquirer* type viewers.

The impact of this is being felt in more than just the United States too. It is becoming a worldwide phenomenon for competitive sports. Anyone who doubts this has only to look at the increase in the amount of coverage being given to American sports in foreign markets.

Whether it is NFL football being played in London or American-style baseball in Tokyo, the American television sports format has become enormously successful in many of the industrialized nations, not only in the West but also in the East.

The world Little League championship almost always has a great team from Taiwan, and they frequently win the championship tournament against teams from every continent.

(I emphasize the East in this because this is not just a Western happening. The Communist world of Eastern Europe is also being impacted, as are the newly industrializing nations of the Pacific Rim, including the Peoples' Republic of China. Remember "ping pong diplomacy"?)

Olympi-drama

The 1980 Olympic Games in Moscow and the 1984 Olympic Games in Los Angeles were much more than the usual quadrennial amateur athletic competition among nations. They were also premiere media events, significant political events, and high profit financial events.

Both of these latest summer games created instant television stars. The audience "love affair" with Nadia Komeneche from Romania in 1980 was followed in 1984 by the instant radiance of America's own Mary Lou Retton and her triumphant smile. That smile has lingered in the hearts of Americans and on our television sets through numerous advertisements for products since that time. In 1988 there will be another instant star.

In both cases, television has created an image, a role

model, of beauty and excellence for youth to see and about which to dream. Both Nadia and Mary Lou have turned out to be excellent role models. They may have become Olympic Gold Medalists through their talent and determination, but they were created as stars by television and by the dramatic need for stars.

There were also millions in profits. The NBC contract to cover the Moscow Summer Games was absolutely staggering. And it reinforced the belief by many that the Kremlin has some extremely astute capitalists in its employ.

And no known sports event in history has made the kind of profits that were seen in Los Angeles. They were so far beyond what even the organizers had dreamed possible that the hints for moving the 1988 games back to Los Angeles if there is trouble in Seoul, South Korea, have more than a little economic motivation to them.

The stage of the television Olympi-drama is an excellent setting for politics as well. Jimmy Carter's boycott of Moscow in 1980 and the Kremlin's response in 1984 both demonstrated the power of the media, and an understanding of how to use events created for one purpose to dramatize issues of another.

The media carried the message in a setting that provided far better coverage—higher visibility for a longer period of time—than if it had been done in a normal political context.

Normal political statements are delivered in the form of a speech, an official statement or a written message. This is at most a 48-hour news story.

Conversely, the Olympic stories in both the 1980 and 1984 cases consumed months of lengthy prime time news coverage continuing all during the pre-Olympic events, during the games themselves and re-covered during the post-Olympic weeks of wrap-up. It was for the protagonist and the media, as they say, a marriage made in heaven.

The ultimate tragedy of the politicization of the Olympic Games was the horrifying massacre in Munich in 1972 of the Israeli athletes. It was pure "terror-vision"—terrorism aimed at getting worldwide television coverage of grievances that had absolutely nothing to do with the Olympics, sports, Munich or the individual athletes themselves. It was a sad day for sports and for humanity.

It has unfortunately made security a major component of every Olympic Game to follow. And the 1988 Summer Games in Seoul already show the signs that South Koreans understand how to get the attention of their government by utilizing the Olympic setting to force changes in their society through televised world opinion.

Rules of Play

Television has also changed the rules of play. The time out is no longer just a matter of the flow of the game, it is now an integral part of the commercial aspect of the game. The "commercial break" for television advertisers is standard fare in all televised athletic events. After all, how else would the schools get the revenues? This has strategic consequences for teams and individual competitors. It affects concentration, timing, momentum and closing.

The game is now played more for the invisible audience of television viewers than for the assembled crowd in the stands. In fact, the assembled crowd of fans can actually be

viewed as part of the backdrop or the scenery of the event—
the event being a television spectacular.

Television has its own set of rules for success in this
as well. As was observed two decades ago by Marshall
McLuhan, the "medium is the message" with television.
This means that the peculiar nature of this two-dimensional,
25-inch square image being beamed into the living rooms of
the audience all across the globe via satellite, cable or local
feed, determines and restricts what can work and what
cannot as a commercial venture, and athletics today is unfortunately all too often a commercial venture.

Football, for example, has been called the perfect television sport. It involves a large playing field, two distinct lines
of players who are easily recognizable from one another but
yet both on camera at the same time, a set drill that is easy
for the audience to follow and time for instant analysis
between plays to assist the audience in enjoying the plays
again. Then it gives a breather to allow the audience to get
back into the next play without being rushed. This allows
better armchair quarterbacks, and subconsciously contrib-
utes to audience draw.

Unfortunately, not many sports have fared so well. Many
sports other than football, in fact, are very dynamic when
seen in person, but look dull and uninteresting on television.

Wrestling is an exciting, competitive sport. It teaches
lessons about practice, hard work, goal-orientation and
success. Likewise it teaches lessons about the discipline and
determination needed to be a winner. I love it. But television wrestling is not a sport; rather it is theatrical violence
disguised as competitive wrestling. Apparently, the networks think that real wrestling is not a TV sport. That's too

bad. There is no sport in the world that requires more physical and mental stamina, concentration, skill and the will to win than wrestling.

Sports Funding

The broadcast media has also changed the funding nature of sports. Again, college football is probably the best example of where millions of dollars are at stake in television rights, broadcast contracts and media markets.

Successful football programs at the privileged few colleges and universities virtually fund the entire athletic program for men's and women's sports, including facilities and expenses. A winning season also is directly correlated with large donors giving to virtually every program on campus.

Television contracts guarantee success by providing the extras that are so attractive to the potential freshmen who are deciding which school to attend. It is hard for Quad Tech Community College to compete with Oklahoma even though the educational benefits may be equal and the costs less.

For the few at the top, television also acts as a sales and promotional tool. It is difficult to compete with the allure of being on television—something every high school athlete and particularly every high school football player dreams of when he watches the top twenty teams play game after game on television every Saturday from late August through early January.

Unfortunately, the opposite is also true. No matter how great a sports program may be, if a team happens to be unlucky enough to be in the wrong media market, the dollars it receives for televising its games—if there are any at all—ensure that it will remain a second class team. The first class Brigham Young University team playing in Provo, Utah, will never receive the same attention or dollars as the first class UCLA team in the rich and populated Los Angeles media market.

Because of the television dollars, it was an intelligent business decision for Arizona State University and the University of Arizona to leave the Western Athletic Conference of secondary media markets in Salt Lake City, New Mexico, Wyoming and west Texas and join the PAC 10, with major media markets in San Francisco, Portland, Seattle and Los Angeles.

The power teams from powerful media markets such as Los Angeles, New York, Philadelphia, Miami and Oklahoma City receive enough money to qualify them for semi-pro status. Schools in these areas are becoming nothing less than farm teams for the NFL. I expect that this disparity will not only continue into the future, but that it will accelerate.

This puts enormous pressure on the NCAA as the successful schools demand greater independence and the rest demand a greater share of the pie. The tragedy of Southern Methodist University is, in part, a direct result of this internal conflict, as are some of the other grudge rules imposed by the majority against the successful minority.

This is true of other sports as well. A good basketball season can bring a million dollars to a school. A season that is just better than average, however, can cost the school that much in lost television contract revenues. A poor season is cause for a coach's professional extinction. The alumni, after all, also watch television.

Everywhere, but especially in the major media markets, a winning coach is considered a hero. So, in addition to what he can get paid by the institution, there are commercial opportunities such as automobiles, personal television and radio shows and other business ventures which can profit from his "star" status.

These are pressures never faced by college coaches before. It affects recruiting, coaches' salaries, placement opportunities in the professional leagues and team morale. Most importantly, however, it can affect the relationship of a coach with his team, and a standout athlete with his peers.

College is a time for learning, yet many times the athletes get short-changed. In the drive to succeed on the field, the coach, faculty, fellow students and fans forget the off-the-field growth that is so essential to maturity and individual happiness. The recent antics of many professional athletes would seem to demonstrate that they too lack the well developed sense of values that successful coaching at the amateur level can impart. I will never understand how these players can claim to be "professional" when their behavior is so boorish.

Television and the Individual Athlete

Another change is that television makes national heroes of individual athletes rather than their remaining just college heroes to the local fans. Names such as Vinnie Testeverde and Doug Flutie were household names long before they reached the NFL. The same is true of Ralph Sampson and Kareem Abdul-Jabaar. And football's Bo Jackson and baseball's Danny Ainge are well known in a sport they didn't want to play professionally.

This places enormous pressure on college athletes before many are ready for it. In some cases it even ends their college careers early as they seek the riches being offered, and forgo an education and career preparation.

Such publicity is bound to have an effect on the athlete's motivation to study and learn, to resist the temptation to claim family hardship, to go for the big money contract, and to receive the maturing benefit of a college education.

It magnifies the gift of the student in one area only to hide the needs in another. This is particularly worrisome in that only a very few college athletes—even great ones—will have a career in professional sports. And those who do seldom have a career in sports that lasts longer than five years.

This means that from age 18 to 25 the athlete must make most if not all the money he and his family need to take them from age 25 to 75. Not only are the odds very long against doing that, it also leaves them unprepared for this Information Age society, and without the knowledge and skills necessary to live a productive, financially rewarding and satisfying life. There is, after all, life after ice hockey or baseball or any other sport.

It is also the largest contributing factor to many of our greatest sports tragedies, as good people struggle with fame and adulation for which they are unprepared. The result can be more than a sports tragedy, it can be a human tragedy.

I find that meaningful coaching in this environment is

especially difficult. Trying to help the athlete improve his skills at the same time as he is viewing himself as a star is most trying. "Olympic Gold-itis" is a disease from which some never recover—and which prevents their ever achieving the potential that could bring them the real Olympic Gold.

Recruiting by professional sports organizations and major universities is just as heavy for winning coaches as for winning players. And the money that can change hands is astronomical.

This is highly disruptive for a college athletic program, and creates uncertainty for coaches and athletes in direction, leadership, methods and consistency. The University of Southern California's football program is instructive. A long string of national championship teams and Heisman Trophy winners was broken when two coaches were back to back lured into NFL by big money: John McKay to Tampa Bay and John Robinson to the Rams. The USC Trojans are just beginning to get their program rebuilt after five lean years.

All this places a burden on the institution, coach and player alike to perform for the school—but also for the dollar. This is far from what those great sports legends Y. A. Tittle, Knute Rockne and Jumbo Elliott had in mind as they roamed the countryside in search of good athletes who wanted to compete for competition's sake. Those were the days.

Chapter III

The American Citizen Athlete

V̲OLUNTARISM is deeply planted in the American character. We believe that people should be "anxiously engaged
in a good cause" for the pure joy of doing, and without regard
for any reward beyond that. This is central to our religious
literature, and it is part of our national culture. It began in
1607 in Jamestown as the first colonists sought voluntarily to
govern themselves. Thus democracy was born.

This is central to our creed. Even as the United States
of America has been good to us by providing the Horn of
Plenty in a land at peace, so should we give back some of
what has been given to us. This has been taught me by my
parents in much the same way as it is taught by parents in
millions of homes in America each day.

Giving is a part of everyday life. Our churches, our
civic organizations and our charitable institutions are all

basically volunteer organizations. From the volunteer fire departments to the all-volunteer Army, we are a nation of individuals who selflessly give of self for the benefit of others, our communities and our country.

Even our political process is managed primarily by volunteer time and talent. From local politics to national campaigns, there are very few political professionals. Most are homemakers, local businessmen and women, workers and other volunteer politicians. A nation governed by representatives of the people, and in which individual representation is essential, requires the sacrifice of time, talent and other resources of the people to succeed. Consequently, this sacrifice makes for excellence on the part of those who do participate. This is their reward.

There are many other examples of voluntary action among our people where their efforts changed lives. The Peace Corps volunteers come as close to selflessness as can be found. For twenty-five years they have been volunteering their lives and talents without any thought of return. This is typical of the American citizen and praiseworthy in any nation.

Sports are another excellent example of the spirit of voluntarism. In many countries of the world—including the Soviet Bloc countries—athletes who train for world-class competition such as the Olympics receive pay and benefits that we would consider makes them professionals. Many other countries do the same.

In the United States, on the other hand, our people still believe that our athletes should compete as the original Greek Olympians envisioned, with the only reward being victory or personal satisfaction. True, for a few there are monetary rewards after the Gold Medal, but even for them there is no gold during the years of training and competition that lead up to the Games. We pride ourselves on amateur status and on the moral confidence this gives us in world competition. We believe that the rules were set for a wise purpose and that to violate even the spirit of the rules robs us of the moral courage required to accept the level of commitment and pain necessary to succeed.

The Foxcatcher Spirit

Team Foxcatcher was created and continues today in this same spirit. It is an example of the dedication to the citizen athlete that produces champions on and off the mat.

It really began with my father who lived in Montpelier, Virginia, in his younger years. That is also the home of President James Madison, author of the U.S. Constitution and the fourth President of the United States of America. In 1905 or so, my Dad acquired a pack of foxhounds and began training them on his farm in Virginia. They became the basis for his sporting interest in fox hunting.

In 1916 my mother's father purchased a farm in Pennsylvania called Liseter Farm. Later, in 1919, when my parents married, they came there to live. Dad called it Foxcatcher Farm and made it the center of our lives. As a wedding present, my paternal grandfather, William du Pont, Sr., had built on the farm a replica of President Madison's home in Montpelier. (Incidentally, that house was designed by President Thomas Jefferson.)

I grew up on these farms. They have always been my

home, and as a boy I saw here the potential to do something very special for other athletes. Even as I cleared running trails and training areas for myself, I knew that someday I would be able to do the same for others. It was more than idle interest, *it was my responsibility.*

All this crystalized in my mind because of the joy and sense of accomplishment I received from being part of the Santa Clara Swim Club. There I saw what could be accomplished and how to do it. We pioneered techniques of training and physical development that proved successful time and again for the athletes in and out of the water. The Santa Clara Swim Club built an allegiance and camaraderie among coaches, staff and athletes that was remarkable. It remains so today. This is the only club for which I have ever competed, and I continue as a Director and member today.

My greatest moment in life was when I stood on the winning block on foreign soil and heard our National Anthem. It made me proud to be an American, proud of my heritage, and grateful for the labors of others that made it possible. With this as a background and training experience, I was determined, when my father passed away in 1965, to do for others what had been done for me. Foxcatcher Farm, now mine from my father, would become a center for voluntary athletic competition. I began by constructing a facility with a competition-sized swimming pool and a gymnasium.

In 1971 a shooting range was completed in the same building as the swimming area. This was subsequently changed into what is now the Foxcatcher wrestling room. Today, this wrestling center is home for the finest wrestling athletes in the world.

In addition to the swimming and wrestling competitors, the Foxcatcher facility is also the headquarters for training athletes in the modern pentathlon, triathlon, track (particularly cross country) and gymnastics. We plan to add to the existing facilities, and to create facilities for other sports, as time and proper staffing permit.

We do not select our athletes. They select themselves. Our philosophy has always been that anyone with any kind of talent is welcome. Ultimately, their own talent and desire will separate them into champions and competitors. Our job is to make their own choices possible. The rest is up to them.

Twenty years of *Team Foxcatcher* has made a significant contribution. Thousands of our athletes have gone on to compete in every part of the world. A few years ago when swimming was highly competitive in this area, there were more than 300 swimmers training here.

Among the Foxcatcher family of athletes, we can now count Olympians, national champions and world champions. The championships are too numerous to count, but at the recent Pan American games our athletes won three gold medals for wrestling and two more for swimming, to add to the two gold medals won at the Pan Pacific Games. Our teams have participated in competition on every continent except Antarctica, and I have little interest in finding out who's there.

We currently have several hundred athletes in training at Foxcatcher. And on staff, in addition to me, we have ten coaches. We receive teams from all over the world who come to freshen their skills before competing here in the United States. We hosted teams from several nations before the Pan American Games last summer.

But equally important, we can count, among those who have trained at Foxcatcher, successful attorneys, doctors, corporate executives, teachers and parents. The spirit of *Team Foxcatcher* has spread to homes all across America and throughout the world.

What We Have Learned

I share this because it helps people understand why we are so successful, and what we have learned. In gymnastics, for example, the lessons learned on the mat apply very clearly to life. To be a successful gymnast one must be aware—at all times—of where the center of the mat is and where you are in relation to the four corners. These are the keys to competition. If the gymnast is not aware, but is floating around without direction, this portends failure.

The same is true of life. If we float around without knowing where the center of our life is, and without understanding where the corners are beyond which we cannot go, then we are doomed to failure. Conversely, by knowing where the really important things in our lives are, and by striving to stay close to them, we cannot be stopped from becoming champions in life.

We also understand now more than before what a tremendous feat the early Olympics were. Many of the world records have since been broken because of new techniques in training and conditioning, as well as better equipment and support facilities. We should salute Jesse Owens, Wilma

Rudolph, and other greats for having succeeded without having had all these advantages.

Equally important, this example should provide us with the determination to see that we create opportunities for every athlete in America who dreams of being an Olympian, or who sees in himself or herself the same spark of greatness that transformed this nation of immigrants into the greatest bastion of freedom and free expression in history. America is home to the millions who voluntarily came here and to their children who voluntarily give of themselves for others and for their nation.

Chapter IV

When Good Guys Mess Up

ALL the talent, all the ability, all the training and all the coaching in the world can make a man or woman a great and champion athlete, and yet still leave the person a failure in life. *Failure*. I don't even like to use that word because it almost never, ever needs to be an accurate description of a person's life.

The truth is, however, that even the good guys and gals in sports mess up; and when they do, it's usually a colossal tragedy. What failings of character or of will cause these tragedies? The question perplexes and saddens me. If I had to assign any single cause it would probably be the *lack of moral fibre and discipline*. Failure to maintain the required levels of intellectual, moral, physical and psychological discipline necessary to live championship lives on and off the mat is the single greatest reason why these character failings happen. The impact is probably magnified also by the athlete's previous high levels of success. The rapid swing and the stark contrast both sharpen the pain of the failing and intensify our sense of shock and disbelief about it. Consider, for example, the case of Len Bias.

At 22 years of age, young Len Bias was on top of the sporting world. An All American basketball player from the University of Maryland, he had been chosen ten minutes into the first round of the NBA draft by the Boston Celtics. Bias was known to dream of playing for the Celtics. His talent and ability were enormous. Even as a rookie player, he attracted admiration and respect from professional veterans in the game. Within hours of being drafted by the Boston team, Bias had also reached an endorsement agreement with a major manufacturer of sports shoes, an agreement that had the potential for providing him with financial security for life.

Yet a scant 40 hours after being on top of the sporting world, financially secure, and chosen by the team of his dreams, young Len Bias lay dead in the emergency room of a Maryland hospital. The verdict was stark and simple, yet chilling: *cardiorespiratory arrest induced by cocaine.* Friends and family, stricken with grief, could not believe the cause of this promising young man's untimely death. Spectacular promise was thwarted by even more spectacularly poor judgment or indifference to the warnings about cocaine's dangers. And, unbelievably, young Bias' death did not seem to have any impact on other promising young athletes.

Twenty-three-year-old Don Rogers, like Len Bias, was on top of the sporting world. A free safety for the Cleveland Browns football team, he had been All American at UCLA

44

in 1983, and the following year he was named the AFC Defensive Rookie of the Year. Yet a scant two weeks after Bias' tragic death, Rogers too lay dead. Twenty-four hours prior to his wedding, the young athlete, blessed with so much promise and so much hope, apparently became the victim of a cocaine overdose that left his lungs and vital organs congested with blood. His UCLA roommate starkly capsuled the tragedy that was Rogers' death when he said, "I was supposed to be a groomsman in his wedding . . . now I'll be a pallbearer at his funeral. . . ."

In 1986 young Dwight Gooden, at 22, was the star pitcher for the World Series winner New York Mets baseball team. He had won the 1985 Cy Young Award and was Rookie of the Year. He too was on the top of the sports world.

But cocaine abuse took him out of the 1987 starting game and put him into a rehabilitation program. His entire career and baseball eligibility were on the line. Gooden's troubled life, perhaps unlike that of Bias and Rogers, had left clues that he was having problems. He missed picking up his Cy Young Award at the awards banquet. He missed the Mets' Victory Parade, a tickertape extravaganza after the World Series. He had several well-publicized run-ins with the police in several areas of the country. And yet, there seemed to be great shock and surprise when Gooden's cocaine problems came to public light.

The stories go on and on. Michael Ray Richardson of the New Jersey Nets had similar problems with drugs. Young Pelle Lindbergh of the Philadelphia Flyers Hockey Team was dead at 26, killed in an automobile crash where alcohol played a role. And what of Alexis Arguello? He is one of only eight men to win world boxing championships in three divisions, and the *only* man never to lose *any* of his titles in the ring. At 31 years of age, he quite literally crashed, lost the millions of dollars he had won in boxing, and entered a life of dissolution and dissipation.

Why do such tragedies occur? How can such promise, such potential and talent be turned to ashes? To me it seems that, while there is no simple answer, the overriding explanation must be *the lack of moral fibre and the lack of moral leadership* in these young athletes' world and in their training and experience. It is a natural tendency for young people to experiment with things that have an element of mystery or danger to them like cocaine. Nevertheless, it is our responsibility as coaches to warn them and to counsel them in clear, but non-threatening, style about the real and inherent dangers posed by drugs. *Please note, not by drug abuse, but by any drug use.* This task is not made any easier by the ready presence of these drugs in our society or by the use of such drugs as steroids and painkillers in athletics.

Second, as coaches and good citizens, we have got to start speaking out about moral abuses in America, whether in business, athletics, the arts or politics. Without becoming moralistic, we must clearly state what we stand for and why, and make it apparent that life's choices have moral as well as practical implications. If they could, what would Len Bias or Don Rogers tell us from beyond this life about the practical, as well as the moral, implications of cocaine use?

And yet, if an athlete messes up with drugs, alcohol, point shaving or whatever and *doesn't kill himself or land in jail,* does he deserve another chance? Circumstances vary, but basically I think the answer is "Yes." And while coaches and teams can help, while psychiatrists and physicians can treat, and other professional counsellors can work with a student athlete with problems, the desire to solve the problem must

46

emanate from and be constantly kindled by the athlete himself or herself.

I do not subscribe to the popular notion that when a kid messes up, it's "society's fault." I believe in, try to live by, and advocate the notion of *individual responsibility for individual actions*. I have seen too many champions who came from the dregs and too many of the privileged who squandered their many resources to believe otherwise. My answer to the nostrum of, "Well, after all, this young man (or woman) has a lot in his (or her) background that has caused this behavior," is to say, "Overcome!!" If professional help is needed, let's get it, but don't let the fact that help is needed excuse or explain away the problem. Professional assistance is a remedy for the problem; the absence of it is not the cause of the problem.

So, yes, good guys and gals do mess up, often spectacularly. If there are pieces around to pick up, then pick up and march on. Better still, coaches need to devote time and energy to providing the moral leadership both on and off the mat to assist athletes to have the moral fibre to persevere in the face of adversity and temptation.

Chapter V

"Hey, Coach"

I WAS preoccupied as I crossed the court toward the fieldhouse. It was very early in the morning, and as a coach, I had a lot to do to get ready for the morning practice. But my eye caught on the statue of a great and beloved man and I stopped. It was the memorial statue of that great coach and friend, James "Jumbo" Elliott, Villanova's towering track and field legend.

"Hey, Coach," one of my athletes said to me as I paused to look at the bronze likeness of Jumbo. "What are you staring at?" he asked curiously.

"Oh, nothing," I answered noncommitally. But my heart was full. For as he said, "Hey, Coach," I heard myself saying the same thing to Jumbo Elliott many years ago when I was "the kid" and he was "the coach." I paused just a moment longer in respect and we walked on together in private thought.

51

There is a lot more to "Hey, Coach" than there is to "Hey, Dan" or "Hey, Fran." Coach is a title of respect, an implicit recognition of authority and friendship. While conferred by some institutions, it really must be earned. It carries with it a great, even sobering, responsibility to lead by example and precept whether it is given to the parent who coaches part-time with the Little League, or a 1,000 percent professional like the great football coach Vince Lombardi. Coach means something.

Whether on or off the mat, on or off the field, I have always believed that coaching is about life, not just about a particular sport. That is something I learned from my coach, Jumbo Elliott. He understood what coaching is all about, and he taught it to me. I have always tried to follow that great example in my coaching life as well.

Over the years I have found that most frequently the problems faced by the student athletes fall into three or four major and distinct categories. First, the student isn't doing well in school. Grades are poor. That's easy to check out. Second, the athlete is having problems with his or her parents, and that is eating away at the back of the mind. Third, the athlete is having girlfriend or boyfriend problems. These too can usually be fairly easily discovered. Unfortunately after that about the only other problem is drug and alcohol abuse, and that one can be very tricky to conquer. Substance abuse can have any number of root causes, and it almost always calls for professional medical and psychological assistance for the athlete to overcome it. But it also calls for a coach's love, concern and compassion.

So often I have found the athlete may turn to me for help when I least expect it. I remember vividly the ease of one of our star competitors in the triathlon. She competed well on the national level, but for a variety of reasons, between the intensity of competition and outside pressures, she had a complete nervous breakdown. She didn't want to swim with anybody. She didn't want anyone to see how far she had fallen. She almost became a total human loss. But she did turn to me for help, even though I really did not know her very well. I took her under my wing when nobody else wanted her. It took over a year, but as we worked together as coach and athlete she was slowly able to regain her self-confidence.

It wasn't just what I did for her, but what the entire triathlon team was able to do for her as well that brought her back. The team literally took her out and dragged her up and down the pool, pumped the highways on bikes with her, and ran with her. We did things together and rebuilt her confidence. She finally got back into competitions, smaller triathlons. Here was a person who had competed for the national championships back at the bottom rung of the ladder. She and I both got a lot of criticism for just that. We ignored that criticism, rebuilt her confidence, and now she is able to compete again. Today she is a champion.

So, when an athlete comes up and says, "Hey, Coach," I listen. I know that the coach on the other end better be listening because he is high on the athlete's level of trust.

Level of Trust

People often ask me why an athlete will turn to a coach first when trouble comes, instead of to a family member or to a minister, priest, rabbi or counsellor. I think most athletes know that a good coach is there to help and not to browbeat the athlete, particularly when there is some problem external to the particular sport.

Often the coach may learn of the problem indirectly from other members of the team. Athletes tend to trust other athletes, so it is not surprising that they are most likely to trust their teammates with sensitive information or problems on the basis of "from my lips to your ears" only. Because they are going through similar experiences, their teammates are able to empathize and offer sympathy and expressions of solidarity.

But while this safety net is vital to keep the kid from feelings of total isolation, it only deals with the first part of the problem: problem identification. Equally important, someone must help the athlete frame the issue, define the alternatives and instill the necessary faith in the athlete that the problem can be solved by him. Enter the coach, the second most trusted person to complete the process: problem resolution.

As the coach then I am the person who must willingly, even anxiously, assume the responsibility for utilizing all the skills and experiences I have developed over the years to begin the process of guiding the student back to success with whatever problem he or she faces.

It is the wise coach who understands that almost every problem can be solved by the individual himself. Most young people today have received the values, education and experience at problem-solving to work through the process to a solution. What they don't have at the moment is objective perspective. They are all caught up in the emotion of the moment, and many times blow up the problem all out of proportion.

William du Pont, a great American citizen, patriot, all around winner at life, and father of John E. du Pont.

John E. du Pont at the 1971
Canadian National Modern
Pentathlon Championship in
Edmonton, Canada.

1976 United States Olympic Team members (left to right), J. du Pont,
K. McCormick, R. Nieman, J. Fitzgerald, M. Burley, D. Johnson.

Young John E. du Pont, representing the United States in the Modern Pentathlon competition in Australia.

John E. du Pont and Jean Austin du Pont join President Gerald R. Ford, a close friend, collegiate All-American football player, and great American citizen athlete.

John E. du Pont has devoted eighteen years of community service as a volunteer law enforcement officer.

A dedicated public servant and volunteer law enforcement officer, John E. du Pont joins in a winter midnight manhunt.

John E. du Pont and fellow swimmer and seven-time Olympic gold medal winner Mark Spitz.

A devoted American defender of freedom and an outspoken advocate of the duty of athletes to be good citizens, John E. du Pont frequently speaks to government, civic, and youth groups.

John E. du Pont and President Ronald Reagan, former life guard and collegiate football player.

John E. du Pont, citizen, patriot, coach, and athlete.

John E. du Pont and his mother, Jean Austin du Pont, congratulate world distance runner Sydney Maree at the 1984 Jumbo Elliott Invitational Track Meet. John presented Maree with an American flag when he became a U.S. citizen.

British Prime Minister Margaret Thatcher receives John E. du Pont on a visit to 10 Downing Street, London. As a champion of America and freedom, John has visited leaders throughout the world.

John E. du Pont meets with Anwar Sadat, President of Egypt.

John E. du Pont hosts Vice President George Bush, a distinguished public servant and former Yale baseball star. They are joined by John's ninety-year-old mother, Jean Austin du Pont.

John E. du Pont escorts President Gerald R. Ford on a walk to Villanova University wrestling practice.

A few of the Team Foxcatcher *athletes, after another swimming meet victory. John E. du Pont founded* Team Foxcatcher *and remains its director.*

Foxcatcher coach John E. du Pont enjoys the thrill of victory with Kursten Hanssen, 1987 Womens National Triathlete Champion and long-time Foxcatcher athlete.

Two Olympic coaches intently observe their wrestlers in action. John E. du Pont and Jim Humphrey, Pan-Am Games medal winner and 1988 U.S. Olympic Wrestling Coach.

Neil Buckley of The Haverford School, Haverford, Pennsylvania, joins John E. du Pont after Buckley's 500th wrestling win as head coach.

Assistant Villanova University wrestling coach Rob Calabrese (left), and assistant coach Mark Schultz (right), an Olympic medal winner, give competitive wrestler John E. du Pont some last minute coaching instructions.

Coach John E. du Pont shares the thrill of success with Joy Hansen, one of his athletes, after she finished third in the 1987 Womens National Triathlon Championships.

Champion Foxcatcher swimmer and Olympic medalist Brenda Borg Bartlett gives a hug of affection to her coach, John E. du Pont.

Two American champions enjoy a laugh together: John E. du Pont and Olympic medalist Mark Schultz.

I can vividly recall the problem faced by one of our very best Foxcatcher athletes. He telephoned me one day from Florida and told me he was quitting competition. I asked him why and he said, "Coach, I just don't want to compete anymore." It had been a tough year for him. His girlfriend was riding a bike with him one day and was hit by a car. She was a triathlete, and while she is okay now, she will never be able to compete again. This tragedy just totally took away this young man's sense of direction and purpose. He just did not know what direction he wanted to take. So instead of sticking to something at which he is a proven winner, he was just dropping everything. I urged him to come back to Foxcatcher. Between the triathletes, the swimmers and the rest of us, we could together turn him around. Sadly, he has not yet returned, but I am hopeful he will.

What is really needed is for the coach to be a patient observer in whom the athlete has faith, and who will devote the time in a conducive setting to help the young athlete sort out his own mind about the matter—with some gentle loving guidance along the way.

There are four basic rules that I believe apply to the coach in his role of counsellor:

1. He must understand that he is dealing with an on-going life, one that transcends both sports and the current problem, one that began long before he met the athlete, and one which will go on for many more years. All the experiences the individual has had to that point can be brought to bear on the problem. It is a much larger setting than the problem of the moment.

2. Before helping guide the person to a change in

attitude or behavior, the coach must first deal with what's there.

3. A coach-counsellor must know where the person needs to go to get back on track.

4. He must have the patience, creativity and endurance to move the injured soul gently from struggle to success.

Finally, at the bottom of the level of trust are the athlete's parents. By the time he reaches college age, there are all too often too many barriers to really confessing his innermost thoughts and problems to his parents. After all, the role of parents in many cases has been to protect, discipline, punish and otherwise find negative methods of dealing with problems.

Don't take this to mean that athletes don't love their parents. Rather, it is the natural tendency of young adults to shield their perceived failures from those with whom they have a permanent relationship, i.e. the family. ("Why worry them? They have enough problems of their own. I'm supposed to be an adult now.")

Coaches are much safer. They usually are not judgmental, they have little punishing power and they are trained to motivate athletes on and off the field.

Most importantly, however, a good coach does not feel personally threatened or responsible for the cause of the problem. Most parents feel guilt themselves—as if their child's failure is their own failure. Therefore, the coach is less emotionally involved, and more able to help the athlete deal with the problem.

Golden Teaching Moments

Once the athlete asks the coach for help, the battle is already half won. It shows a recognition of the problem, an acceptance that it is a problem, and a search for a solution. Now, it's up to the coach to recognize this "Golden Teaching Moment" (or GTM) and seize the opportunity.

I call it a Golden Teaching Moment because teaching occurs when the person to be taught opens himself up to the teacher, not when the mood strikes to teach.

Teaching is about the receiver, not the sender. The teacher usually has to find ways to motivate the student to want to learn. But once in a while a student will be sparked to ask a question. That is a Golden Teaching Moment.

This is the same with a coach and student athlete. When the "kid" says, "Hey, Coach. I was wondering if you had a minute," the coach must be instantly aware of both the opportunity and the responsibility. It must be dealt with immediately by arranging the soonest available specific time and place. (No "Let's talk about it sometime." That really means, "Don't bother me with your problems, kid.")

GTM's don't happen very often. But when they do, as a coach I must be prepared to act with the same swiftness as when I pin an opponent to the mat. Victory is a matter of milliseconds, not days.

A Coach, a Father

A coach is a father figure to most athletes, a father away from home for college athletes. And sometimes he is the only father figure. This relationship between coach and athlete is an even more intense one than most students have with their professors or teachers because of the level of personal involvement. A coach and athlete must work together to see the athlete succeed. Others on the campus seldom have the same level of individualized relationship.

A second reason a coach takes on this role more than others is that he must deal with the total self-concept of the athlete, not just his subject matter. Sports is not a subject. It is a discipline: physically, mentally, emotionally. As such, it must be taken as an expression of the total person.

A student can be an excellent math student and still have worrying personal problems. A competitive athlete must have the reserve mental strength to strip away all outside influences during practice and on the mat.

A young swimmer I knew walked into the Santa Clara Swim Club one day a few years ago looking for his coach. When he found him his face showed deep pain, but didn't prepare the coach for the words. "Coach," he said, "last night my mom died. I don't know what to do." Immediately the coach asked, "Where is she?" And, in stunned silence, he heard the boy reply, "Outside in the back seat of my car. I didn't know what to do. So I came here for you." Nothing in life had prepared the coach for this. But he was truly a coach: a person of respect and love. He did his job . . . out of the pool.

It's part of a coach's job. And key to being able to do that job is to listen to the real message being communicated and to understand how to use the role of coach to improve the life of the athlete. Then he must take the time to do it.

As with any bureaucracy, a university has a lot of process work that a coach must do. But he should never let that interfere with his reason for choosing to be a coach in the first place: to help the athlete excel on and off the field of play, to coach winners.

Quitting

A young swimmer called me the other day and said, "Coach, I'm quitting." I know he meant that he had decided not to compete as a swimmer any more, but his voice was really saying, "I'm quitting at life, it's got me, I'm defeated."

It is not uncommon for young people as highly motivated, talented and achievement-oriented as the Foxcatcher and Villanova athletes to feel discouraged—sometimes even to the point of being ready to quit. When anyone strives as diligently to be a champion as our athletes do, there are many times when it seems easier to just quit than it does to go on.

But invariably, before they hit the bottom they call or come see the coach. In almost every case, what they are really saying is not, "I want to quit," they're saying, "I've already quit, help me start again." A good coach can see it in the face, in the eyes, the shoulders, the walk, everything. (It's called body language, and there have been a lot of good books written on the subject.)

What is important in reading body language, however, is knowing what to do once it has been accurately diagnosed. Time is the most important ingredient in re-starting the fire of desire in an athlete. Quality time, surrounded by other winners.

There are many successful approaches. Some coaches have the athlete stay close to them, others see that they stay with teammates. Whatever the method, it is important that the athlete be surrounded by successful others who understand what they have to do to help the other succeed within himself. It is one thing to go onto the mat or in the pool and win, it is a very different matter (and in many ways much more rewarding) to bring someone else back from the bottom and see that person succeed in and out of the pool, on and off the mat.

It is here that a coach truly is tested: on having the ability to motivate other athletes to give of themselves to help a teammate. So much of sports is self-oriented that it is very rewarding to see an athlete become other-oriented. The coach must be other-oriented too, to succeed in instilling this sense of selflessness in his athletes. Sometimes the athlete has already learned and lived this lesson, having been taught it usually by a strong and confident parent. My friend, Vice President George Bush, who played baseball as a young man and later in college, told me that one day he burst into the living room of his parents' home with the news that he had hit a home run at that day's baseball game. "That's very nice, George," his mother replied, "but how did the team do?"

Vice President Bush says that that taught him a valuable lesson—not about baseball—but about winning and about life. It's all attitude. My father, one of America's great citizens and a true competitor, taught me to have a positive mental attitude and thus to be a winner. Like the Vice President's, our efforts at Foxcatcher and at Villanova are team efforts. They are buttressed, to be sure, by strong individual efforts, but it is the unifying efforts of that team spirit that unlock the higher fraction of the human spirit so needed for excellence in any endeavor. The great gurus of business management theory just now seem to be discovering what coaches and athletes have known for years. From the combined efforts of the team come results exceeding the sum of individual efforts, while simultaneously propelling the individual to new levels of achievement. There is a lesson here for all Americans as we seek answers to the difficult and perplexing issues of our times: international competitiveness, the budget deficit, drug abuse, national defense, and so forth. America is a team!

Second Chance

Sometimes an athlete really does fail; it's not just mental fatigue, social problems or health problems. There is a breakdown in the mental toughness necessary to win again. This can happen to champion athletes just as it can happen to up-and-comers.

An excellent athlete came to me a few months ago. A champion. A champion who was defeated—not by the competition, but by herself. In her own mind she was finished.

But I knew better. To me, she was still a champion, a winner. But more important than my knowing it, I knew that she needed to know she was a winner—not for the trophy or the team, but for herself and how she would view herself for the rest of her life. That was my challenge as well as hers.

The rehabilitative process for a torn ligament or a separated shoulder is no different from the rehabilitative process for a torn self-image. It takes time, patience, repetition, building through goal-setting and faith. Lots of faith and caring by others.

It is a team effort. It requires the buccaneer spirit of "all for one and one for all." It takes a coach to lead the effort, bring the people together as one unit, inspire confidence, set the goals with care and give opportunity at the proper level.

This last point is crucial. The athlete must begin competing, but the competition must begin back at the basics and not at the world-class level. Then it must build carefully to put the athlete together again. She has to move from small success to small success. Then from large to larger. Finally, and patiently, she can return to the great successes of a true champion.

The coach needs to always carry the motto, however, that no success on the mat is as important as the ones off the mat in life. There are no words to describe how a coach feels when his triathlete says, "Hey, Coach, thanks for the second chance."

The Real Problem

Several times in this book I have referred to the "real problem." That is because the real problem may not be apparent from what the person says: "I'm just not with it today," "For some reason, I can't seem to do it now," and any number of other non-statements. These are what I call "reaching statements." Deep down inside the athlete he knows he needs and/or wants help. These statements are subconsciously designed as signals to the listener that something is going on that needs closer examination. The perceptive coach will learn to interpret these SOS calls, make a mental note, and follow it up either right then or as soon as it is practical. The goal is to arrive at the real problem.

There is no problem that is unsolvable. I have never met a young athlete with a problem that was terminal. The only thing that is terminal is when the kid reaches out, calls, "Hey, Coach," and there is no real coach in life on the other side.

Chapter VI

"Hey, Kid"

IT TAKES an exceptional coach to be aware enough to hear the cry for help when something becomes so important to an athlete that he recognizes he can no longer "go it alone" and calls out. This recognition alone is a victory.

And I admit it is difficult in the intense situations a coach faces day after day to hear the message. In between the rub-downs, on-the-mat coaching, paperwork, staff meetings, etc., just hearing can get difficult, let alone real listening. (The distinction is that *hearing* is an audio motor skill, *listening* is the mental skill of directing attention to something.)

There was a Broadway play called "The Roar of the Greasepaint." I can't speak to that, but I can say that the "roar" of the mat or the pool can be very loud and consuming. Listening in that environment can get very difficult. Committing to doing something about what is heard requires a supreme effort, but one that pays enormous human dividends.

It is even more difficult, however, to read the signs without being verbally told. The social-psychologists call these attributes "people-reading skills." (This is different from people-directing or motivating skills.)

This is the skill of "reading" the body, the surroundings and the peers without verbal verification. And then making an accurate conclusion or diagnosis of the state of mind or behavior of the person based on these observations.

Some people are born with the talent of people-reading. I have met only a few. Jumbo Elliott was one of them. He not only loved athletes, he was intensely interested in what came out the other end of the educational process, not just at the finish line. His was a talent to read the hidden messages.

As my coach, he had the ability to look at me and see where I was in life at the moment. He knew how to motivate me, and how to show he cared. I felt his love for me as an athlete and as a human being.

It is one thing to be a tough, demanding, fair coach. It is something special to be one who, after a tough session of correction, can show you care. It never hurts to walk up to someone who has just received the lecture of his life from you and say, "Hey, Kid. You're great. Lov' ya, pal." Jumbo could do that.

I try to as well. And I can safely say that I have had no greater reward in life than when I have succeeded here.

Most who possess the skill of people-reading have developed it because of a determination to make a difference, and who have—with the same process by which any other skill is perfected—studied, learned, practiced *and* practiced it until it became a natural part of their awareness.

Learning to "read the signs" like an old Indian tracker takes experience and awareness. It is one of the most important skills that distinguish the coaches who do well only on the mat from the very few who actually excel off the mat as well. It separates excellence from greatness.

It gets exceptionally difficult to deal with an athlete's problems of character. They may have little or nothing to do with performance in the sport. Unfortunately, the problems may result from success in the sport. The "Olympic star" syndrome can be very dangerous to an athlete's proper development.

These problems may not be life or health threatening. But they are character threatening, and unless dealt with carefully and consistently, they can cause permanent damage.

A coach must learn to differentiate between the two problems (problems on the mat and problems off the mat), and treat each differently. The first step is evaluation. There are two ways in which to evaluate a person: character evaluation and performance evaluation.

Performance evaluation looks at how well a person does something; character evaluation studies who and what a person is. Each needs to be analyzed separately.

Performance Evaluation

Performance evaluation is about what happens on the mat or in the pool. It is composed of three evaluative components of the person to the performance of competition: knowledge, skills and abilities.

Knowledge is acquired information necessary to understand how to perform a certain move, behavior or subject. It is an intellectual exercise. It has been called the "textbook learning" about a subject.

For example, *Golf My Way* by Jack Nicklaus, tells the reader about this golf champion's method of playing the game of golf. It provides a mental picture of the skill to be performed by dissecting it into component parts, classifying and analyzing them, and describing them to the reader.

This is the first of three legs of the performance evaluation stool. (As you know, a stool with three strong legs will stand under intense pressure. If one leg is weak, however, the stool will collapse no matter how strong the other two. Therefore, it is a good analogy here.)

Knowledge can only be acquired by intense study. The athlete who cannot study cannot excel. For those who do not excel at studying in the traditional ways, in today's world there are plenty of alternative study methods to make up for it. Computer-assisted learning, video learning and role playing are just a few.

When I was at the Santa Clara Swim Club, for example, I introduced the first video training into the swimming program of an American swimming team. Film had been used for years of games and meets, but this was the first time it had been used as a practice mechanism for the purpose of teaching the athlete on the spot where correction and improvement were needed.

A coach can shout, "Bring your elbow up higher" a thousand times and not get results if the athlete thinks he or she is already doing what's right. But just one video that provides the knowledge to the athlete of an actual performance overcomes all the mental blocks to internalizing the knowledge of what change is required.

Now there are hundreds of video training films being sold in stores on almost every sport. These have replaced book learning for many people, and they provide an excellent knowledge tool for those who have a hard time conceptualizing from the written word.

Skill is the second leg of the stool. Skills are the physical manipulations required for performing a certain action or behavior. They are acquired through repetition. We have all seen the Sea World dolphins perform what the trainer calls "behavior," with a fishy reward. Skill development in humans is essentially the same process. The rewards may be different, but the need for repetition, hands-on correction, slow-motion concentration, speed development and goal-setting are standard components.

Skill demonstrates the knowledge: playing a piano, wrestling on the mat, painting a picture. Each of these is a skill, actually doing it as opposed to talking about it or thinking about it.

They are the "hands-on" adjunct of knowledge. In fact, some people say that the only place where college students get skill training is in the athletic department. And while this is not true, the athletic department certainly must be one of the most visible places where skills are acquired.

Ability is the God-given talent to do something. It is the final leg of a champion's stool. This is what the potential is; to others there is just the potential to compete well.

There is no substitute for determination in life. But in competition, the talent must also be there. I'll never sing like Placido Domingo no matter how determined I am, or how much I study, or how much I practice. I don't have the talent. (But I'll meet him on a mat any day.)

I was once asked if I had ever dropped an athlete because he "didn't have it." I answered, no, I just re-direct them. And fortunately, in athletic competition, because of the hundreds of sports requiring such varied skills as endurance, hand-eye coordination, brute strength and balancing skill, almost no person who is interested in excelling in sports is without the ability to excel in some sport. The Olympics are filled with the most varied sports imaginable, each with its own set of knowledge, skill and ability requirements.

In fact, one of the beauties of sports like the triathlon and pentathlon is that they are the combined skills of multiple sports. Whereas someone may not have the ability to be a champion in any one sport, that same person can have the combined abilities to do very well in each and thereby to be a combined winner.

Knowledge, skills and ability. These are the three parts to performance that a coach must evaluate. In the case of the first two, the coach has the opportunity to teach and improve performance. In the case of abilities, however, the coach can only increase motivation; the rest is up to the individual.

Character Evaluation

Character is the combination of values a person holds, his self-concept, his concept of how he should relate to others, and his evaluation of others. It is demonstrated on and off the mat. It is how the person behaves under any circumstance.

Where performance has everything to do with what goes on during competition, character is the essence of the person both on and off the mat.

The many tragedies of athletes in varying degrees of trouble with the law or, in the extreme, of those who have succumbed to the temptations of drug abuse or alcoholism, offer stark and poignant testimony to flaws of character that rend otherwise whole fabric.

The responsibility to make character evaluations is much more complex than the responsibility to make performance evaluations. It tests both the coach's own character and abilities, and the athlete's readiness to learn and change.

It is a special responsibility that hits at the core of a coach's own values. And it requires the coach to search within himself to find and understand his own beliefs. As is written on the remains of the Temple of Apollo at Adelphi in Greece, "Know Thyself."

Every coach who determined to be more than an on-the-mat coach must apply this test first to himself: "Who am I?" The continuing search for the answer to this primal question is a sacred responsibility and trust that has eternal consequences both for the coach and for the athletes for whom he is responsible. One cannot teach what one is not. If the coach is unwilling to apply the standard to himself, he cannot expect his team to apply it to themselves.

Courage has been defined as "grace under pressure." In this definition it is grace (the attribute of character), not pressure, that determines the winner. It is what the person is rather than what he does that differentiates the person of courage from the coward. The same can be said of any evaluation where character plays a part.

A friend of mine told me of an experience he had had that demonstrates this very well—and also why it is ultimately more important than performance even on the mat.

He had been in the Marine Corps Officers' Basic School at Quantico during the Vietnam War. The training had been intense, knowing as each lieutenant did that he would soon be going into combat.

They were evaluated every day on performance: squad tactics, machine gun fire, air support, rifle assembly and so forth. Nothing escaped notice. At the same time, over a period of five months they also made friends, spent weekends together, and developed into groups of officers who enjoyed the company of some more than others. A natural process of selection happened that is also at work on any campus or in any organization in the world.

At the end of the Basic School training there was a final evaluation that each lieutenant had to pass: peer evaluation. It was the most difficult in that it required each newly commissioned lieutenant to make his first command decision—judge his fellow officers.

There were many, many categories: physical abilities, leadership, decision-making skills, dress and moral character, to name a few. But, he said, the one that really counted was the question which came at the end of the evaluation, after all the usual questions had been asked: *"Would you want this person to serve as the commanding officer of the platoon on your right flank in combat?"*

Imagine having to face such a question. At that moment all the normal pressures to "vote for your friends" (that come naturally in high school and college class president elections) were meaningless. Popularity, talent, looks and other attributes that are—in the final analysis of life—really secondary became meaningless to him. All that was important was character. This was character evaluation at its best. It stripped away all unimportant issues. And few friendships were strong enough to stand up to this moment of truth.

I have always believed that even if an athlete wins in performance, if he fails in character then he will ultimately be judged a tragedy. Long after the wrestler is gone, the character of the person lives on.

There are too many stories of the heroes of yesteryear who do not have the character to be the daily heroes of life. These are the stories of human tragedy. Chapter Four looked at a few examples of this. Unfortunately, there are too many for any one book.

Conversely, many whose performances on the field were only good (as distinguished from champion-like) have become the bulwarks of America off the field. The corporate officers, and professional, religious and political leaders who have graduated from college after playing amateur sports have provided America with leadership that understands excellence, sportsmanship, competition and grace under pressure.

This is what the coach's purpose is: to produce winners on and off the field of play. But if either is to take second place it must be on the field. The NCAA was created for this purpose, and its sanctions are for the most part both just and wise for the long-term benefit of the athletes as human beings.

This means that the coach must be part of the educational

system of the university, not an adjunct to it. Its purpose is not just to impart facts, it is to teach values, and the facts that accumulate on them form the basis of education. And knowing how and when to step in as a coach into this value base of the athlete is the mark of greatness in the coach. It is, in a very real sense, an evaluation by the coach of his own character.

Chapter VII

Teaching
Stewardship

ATHLETIC programs are only a few of the many diverse offerings at a college or university. And although for most participants and spectators alike athletic events are an exciting part of campus life, they are not the "end all" for them. Believe it or not, there really is life after basketball season.

Further, very few good college athletes take their sport seriously enough to expect to continue on professionally. And fewer make it.

Of course the same thing can be said for the other activities available to students on campus. But there really is something special—something unique—about the bonding that takes place at college athletic events. It performs its magic on the entire school, the community in which it is housed, and the surrounding circle of "family" who make up College Town, USA.

To each of these circles of College Town family, the athletes themselves are seen as representing each one of these groups and each individual in it. It is as if more than a team is playing and more than an athletic victory is at stake. David is facing Goliath again, and the winner takes all.

This representativeness is an important social phenomenon for a school. It is a statement about the institution itself and all who are associated with it. It brings people together for a common cause, it provides common expectations for success, and it places the individual athlete in a position of respect and hope.

This is not always easy for an athlete to understand or cope with. Not all are prepared for the social responsibility that accompanies success on the mat. They have not been taught correct principles (or perhaps better said, not taught at all) and consequently do not have the value-based foundation to assist them in making correct decisions.

Coaches must understand and respect this. But more importantly, we have an absolute imperative early on to teach fundamental principles to our athletes before the false standard of self-importance is erected by the athletes themselves, based on the typical BMOC treatment they receive from their peers. Their friends off the mat are much more a problem than their adversaries on the mat.

The Principle of Stewardship

Citizenship is one of those responsibilities that must be taught to every athlete; but it is only one of several concepts that is based on a more fundamental (or founding) principle called *stewardship.* Among the others are a love of nature, a respect for property and a sense of community. The Founding Fathers named life, liberty and the pursuit of happiness.

The idea of stewardship is a critical concept to get across to young athletes (and all Americans, for that matter) in this nation: we are stewards on this earth, not masters. We all walk on Mother Earth together. It has been granted to us as a trust; but it belongs to Him.

We believe that we own parts of this World. I consider that my own Foxcatcher Farm is mine. And, according to the laws of the United States of America, it is. In a broader sense, however, when I pass on, it will pass into the hands of others—and others after that. In the same way, it belonged to the Indians long before it came to our family.

The permanent hands that hold it are His, and all shall be returned to Him in the end. Hopefully, Foxcatcher Farm will be better for my having tended it.

We are the stewards. And a steward is one who has responsibility to care, to tend, to nurture, to improve and to report back to Him from whom the stewardship was granted. An accounting will be made, and each will account for his time as a steward.

Stewardship in America

In America this is what we expect of our elected leadership. They are the stewards of our nation—a stewardship granted by WE THE PEOPLE for a limited time. This gives our leaders a special position of trust.

That trust is to be exercised by the leaders on behalf of WE THE PEOPLE as if the people were exercising it themselves. And, at a specific time, each must be held to an accounting. We call this process an election or re-election.

This is very different from most governments of the world where something called "divine right," "the state" or "the Party" is the grantor of the stewardship. We recognize no such authority to grant rights to government. In fact, we specifically reject such an authority.

Here in America, because of the unique relationship we have between the representatives and WE THE PEOPLE, the same principle of stewardship is inherent in the responsibility of the individual citizen. WE THE PEOPLE also pledge ourselves to uphold and defend the Constitution of the United States of America against all enemies both foreign and domestic. And we pledge "allegiance to the Republic" which means to each other and those we elect to represent us.

This is why the right to bear arms is so important. We are the defenders of our nation. Our armed forces are an extension of the people, not of the government. As a close reading and study of our Constitution will demonstrate, the Founding Fathers inserted the "right to bear arms" clause in support of citizen militias in the various states. During the period immediately preceeding the American Revolution, efforts had been made to make the colonists pay for quartering foreign troops on American soil, while at the same time denying those colonists the right to form and maintain their own militias. The ultimate responsibility for the defense of America and her ideals and liberties lies with those who granted the power. We the citizens did, and we renew that trust at every election.

I have called our competitive sportsmen and women "citizen athletes." This is because I believe that in the same way that our armed forces are citizen soldiers and our political leadership is composed of citizen politicians, the non-professional athlete is a citizen athlete. His or her reward is not money; it is the satisfaction of knowing that he is the best, a champion.

His accomplishments represent not just individual achievement, but also an American achievement. It has national implications, with long-term consequences.

Our citizen athletes have an important responsibility in demonstrating the principle of stewardship. In a very real sense, whenever they compete at home or in world competition (especially in world competition) they represent all of us as if we ourselves were competing. That is why I brought the Puerto Rican athletes to Valley Forge. I wanted them to realize they were part of our Nation's effort. I help the kids because I want America to win.

A Respect for God

First of all, the good citizen athlete represents a respect for God and for His presence in our daily lives.

This country was founded on the belief that it is "one nation, under God"—a phrase in our Pledge of Allegiance that was placed there by Congress at the insistence of President Dwight D. Eisenhower.

Also, we pray before many of our amateur sporting events. Usually the prayer is for the nation, the players and clean sportsmanship. Seldom is it for victory—even in private locker rooms. Rather it is to compete to potential, avert injury and return with dignity regardless of the outcome.

Additionally, our coins note that "In God We Trust." This is an essential belief of our nation that is not shared in many places of the world. It sets the American form of government apart from many different systems in nations of the world that reject the Divine in favor of the State. I once saw a bumper sticker that read: " 'God Is Dead,' (signed) 'Nietzsche.' 'Nietzsche Is Dead,' (signed) 'God.' " That puts it in perspective.

We Americans have a deep and abiding commitment to and respect for God. Every Sabbath when I am walking alone here on my farm, I cannot help but look in wonder at the beauty and grace that God has given this land. God has indeed "shed His grace on thee" in this land of America.

One Nation

Next, our athletes represent our nation. I use the word "nation" rather than "country" or "state" for a very good reason. The word *nation* refers to the people who live in a country. The term "one nation" refers to the unity of spirit that exists in our nation. It has been termed the "sense of comity" among the people.

President Gerald Ford used to remark that just as the beauty of Joseph's coat was its many colors, so is the beauty of the American nation its many peoples. In our ethnic and cultural diversity, we find strength and durability. In our geographic and lifestyle diversity, we bring together an entire nation founded on common principles, opportunity and free exercise of conscience.

Country refers to the physical land. This is the home in which the nation has refuge. We are blessed with enormous natural resources, but so are many other nations. It is the people who have brought us to greatness.

State refers to the government. But in the American experiment, because the government is the creation of and is subservient to WE THE PEOPLE, the state (or government) is secondary and the people reign supreme. This is what is unique about the American experience, what was so revolutionary about the Declaration of Independence, so radical about the Constitution.

Therefore, it is the American nation that is represented. It is the nation of individuals who provide our strength, our sense of moral purpose, our aspirations and our dreams. They represent the American nation. We coaches must teach this to our young athletes.

Team Spirit

Our citizen athletes also represent their team. Whether at a university or a private training facility, each individual is molded into the entire team. When one wins, all rejoice. When one loses, all mourn. It is the wise coach who builds team loyalty as the guiding spirit of his athletes.

A good coach can take average talent and make a winning team. Team spirit—*esprit de corps*—makes that possible.

Call it the "Cinderella Team" or the underdog, the team that plays as a team can overcome the team with one standout.

This is as true of the sports that depend on individual effort (such as wrestling and tennis) as it is on team sports (such as baseball and hockey). The concentration required for victory in all cases can be dramatically enhanced by the support and encouragement of teammates.

Families Are Forever

The basic unit of society is not self, it is family. The family is the most primal organization. All of history is written about the survival instinct of leaders for their family (called "people") rather than of individuals for themselves.

The Torah (also known as the Old Testament) is a family book. It is the founding document of the greatest religion in the world. We may look at it as a book about nations, but it is essentially a family book. Adam and his family. Noah and his family. Abraham and his family.

Their leadership was in terms of family (or patriarchal) leadership. Their stories are family stories. They are very personal and very human. They speak of how they passed from one generation to the next, yet maintained (and built upon) family traditions and experience.

Nothing has changed. Passing the torch to the new generation is the most important step most people will ever take. It has consequences that go far beyond economic security. It is, in the broadest sense, the basis of our civilization.

These are the building blocks of our nation as we add to

the combined knowledge and values of one generation and place them on the altar before the generation that follows.

We must teach our young athletes to remember their families and represent them well. And to prepare for the generation that will follow them.

To Thine Ownself

Finally, each athlete represents himself or herself. This is an ultimate truth. One cannot run from this responsibility, neither can anyone point to someone else. Equally important from the perspective of the coach, the failures of the athlete off the field of play are far more public than the failures of the chemistry student or the computer engineer. In fact, far from being just personal, they are public news. They become public property and are covered in just the same way as their actions on the mat.

This may not be fair. But the coach who does not totally convince his athletes that it is reality will be doing them a disservice from which they may never recover. There are too many examples of good athletes who generated bad publicity and ended up without the support they needed to start again.

A key to overcoming this must be a recognition that success does not happen alone. Neither will happiness come from living with it alone. Someone once said that "Success has many fathers, but failure is an orphan." The greatest failure is not to recognize those who helped achieve the success. This failure is the beginning of years of aloneness.

On the other hand, the striving for excellence in mind, spirit and body, all combined, produces champions. And when combined with proper stewardship, it produces pride, a sense of purpose and direction and the achievement of self-fulfillment.

When an athlete is able to achieve a balance among these components of stewardship, then that person will become truly great no matter what the outcome on the mat or in the pool.

Chapter VIII

Coaching Off the Field

T H E F I R S T obligation of a coach is to prepare the athlete for competition on the field of play. Nothing takes precedence over this. In fact, this is the basis upon which a coach—as coach—will be judged. John Wooden, "Bear" Bryant, John McKay and Angelo Dundee are great names as coaches or trainers because they produced winners. And producing champions is what a coach is expected to do. It is what I as a coach have always tried to do.

Perhaps this is so basic that it doesn't need to be said. It is not a comment about the coach as a human being, or in any of his many other demanding roles. But it is what the coach is hired to do. The criteria for choosing a coach are several, including character. But there is no more important criterion than success. The off-the-field successes of a coach make winners and good citizens for life of the athletes. That's what this book is all about.

But the on-the-field successes continue to make him a coach. Few coaches last long in the business if they can't produce any winners or winning teams. That's as true of sports as it is of any other profession. Ask any three college coaches today how long they would last if they had no victories for three consecutive seasons, and I'm sure the answer would be unanimous: not long.

There are many requirements for coaching winners on the field, but before the athlete can be coached, the athlete himself must have the talent and motivation to want to win—and to be willing to pay the price to win. Without that, no amount of training will make up the difference. Look at our Olympic athletes. At my Foxcatcher Olympic training swimming pool, our athletes are already in training for the 1988 Summer Olympics. They train (swim and condition) an average of six hours a day. Every weekday. That is dedication, and one that is a much higher price than most people would be willing to pay. These athletes know what winning requires, and they are winners at heart.

At the games we all see the smiles of victory. What we don't see are the years of training, and all that was missed in its place. A lady once said to the great cellist Pablo Casals after one of his concerts, "Oh, Mr. Casals, I'd give my life to play the cello like you do." He replied kindly, "Thank you, madam. I did." And so do our Olympic athletes who truly have the desire to achieve victory.

Someone told me that in politics there is nothing worse than the reluctant candidate, no matter how glamorous, wealthy or articulate that candidate may be. The reluctant candidate will not have what it takes when the heat is really on. It is more important to choose someone who is eager to go the distance than someone who feels flattered to be asked, but doesn't see the prize as worth all human efforts.

The same is true of sports. The basic ingredients must be there: talent and determination. If, however, there is to be less of one than of the other, let there be less talent. I'll pick the less talented, more determined athlete every time. And that athlete will be a winner every time.

The reason for this is simple: a champion is a champion in his mind and heart long before it shows up in physical skills. The discipline and concentration required to be a winner during hours, days, weeks, months and years of training are painful, and can be exhausting. This is a matter of character, not talent.

Character is evidenced by commitment, not by intent or by stated desire. It is the follow-through on a daily basis that establishes character. It is the evidence of commitments kept, particularly when it is not convenient, and something else is much more enticing.

Mental Toughness Through Conditioning

Another aspect of commitment to success is the relationship between mental toughness and physical performance. Nowhere is this more evident than in the application of the principle of "playing through pain." Playing through pain is what "separates the men from the boys," as they say. And, it separates the women from the girls, too. Many can be great, but it is the mental toughness to ignore pain and keep on competing that makes the difference. Fortunately (or maybe unfortunately), I know all about playing through pain from firsthand experiences. I have taken in my playing and coaching career over thirty trips to the hospital operating room to deal with injuries or accidents. Yet I still want and intend to keep coaching and to maintain an active lifestyle. I just have to work around injuries and keep on.

Playing through pain is a matter of desire. I've never met a wrestler or any other competitor who had a natural ability to ignore pain. Like green olives, it is an acquired taste. Just like the desire to win, ignoring pain requires the *desire* to ignore pain. From then on, it is just plain hard work.

No athlete goes through his career pain-free. It is a myth that any athlete has an iron body that never gets hurt. We all get hurt. We all feel pain. No amount of physical conditioning can eliminate pain, for it is the very nature of athletic competition to extend the body to its physical limits. And that means pain. Mental desire and mental conditioning make it possible for an athlete to block out the pain—to work through the pain with both eyes on the goal.

Eyes on the Goal

In the very same way, the competitor must also be conditioned to work through the opponent to victory. If all an athlete thinks about is his opponent, he will never achieve victory. Defeating an opponent on the mat is not the ultimate goal; victory is the ultimate goal. Defeating an opponent is only the means to getting to the real goal. Every athlete must be prepared by his coach to understand this, and to keep the ultimate goal in sight at all times. If the competitor is committed to this, then defeating the opponent becomes just a part of the process rather than the end result.

This is important because this is part of the mental conditioning that results in allowing no possibility other than victory to enter the thought process. Once an athlete is defeated mentally, physical prowess and conditioning are superfluous.

There is a lesson for America here, particularly for the Congress as it attempts to pass a budget to serve as a basis for running the Federal government and for spending our tax dollars. The Constitution and our laws mandate that Congress is supposed to pass a budget each year. For at least the past fifteen years, since they "reformed" the budget process, not once, not a single time, has Congress managed to pass a complete budget. Congress should start treating all the special interest groups like wrestling opponents. Get committed to passing a budget, instead of trying to act like 535 Secretaries of State or Defense (or Presidents), and then defeating these special interest groups will just be part of the process of responsible government.

I worked with an athlete once who was a world class champion. He had all the talent, training and desire of a gold medal winner. There was only one flaw: he had been convinced at one time in his career that he could never defeat a particular opponent.

He was stronger than the other. He was more talented. He was better trained. But he was defeated before he stepped onto the field of play. He lost sight of victory every time in his effort to defeat his opponent. He came to lose, his opponent came to win. The power of the mind to direct was at work. Without the constant reinforcement of the visual image of being a winner, of doing what a winner does, and of thinking like a winner thinks, no person can become a winner at any endeavor on or off the mat.

Coaching On the Field

There are several aspects to successful coaching and training. In fact, hundreds of books are written about it each year. Here I would just like to cover a few of the more significant ones that deal with the coach-student relationship.

Physical conditioning. The first is teaching and training in physical conditioning. The body must be prepared to do what the mind commands it to do—exactly, expertly and without hesitation. This requires as much time and commitment on the coach's part as on the athlete's. We must never get so bogged down with bureaucratic busywork that we do not attend to the physical training of the students.

Development of mental toughness. This is taught and should be demonstrated as often as possible for effect. I once saw a demonstration given by a military officer about the use of an antidote to chemical poisoning. He took a needle filled with a liquid out of his pack to demonstrate how to inject oneself with the antidote. Without warning, he pulled off the cover and plunged the needle into his own leg, and continued with the lecture for two more minutes. Then he removed the needle. I have never been so startled by mental toughness as I was that day.

Concentration. Blocking out all distractions is extremely difficult. Yoga, the martial arts and several conditioning exercises all contain as their central thesis the concept of total concentration. The roar of the crowd is an important boost for most athletes. But for the best, there is no crowd, no space outside the perimeters of the mat. There is only oneself, the match and victory. Nothing else exists.

Basics and skill. Every sport has its basic methods and skills to achieve victory. These need to be taught, re-taught, self-analyzed (a video is most helpful) and corrected. When all else fails, get back to the basics. All women and men who have achieved greatness in some field of endeavor, whether in athletics, business, the arts or science have first had to master the fundamentals. Failure to do so results in loss after loss, in frustration and resignation. One of the reasons we so admire the champions of any sport is that they have so thoroughly come to grips with the fundamentals that it becomes second nature to them, leaving them able to concentrate on the strategies needed for winning. The psychologists refer to this mental conditioning as the level of "unconscious competence" in a given field.

Experience and development. Nothing takes the place of experience. Nothing develops skills like having to use them in a competitive environment. As coaches, we need to be particularly aware of the delicate balance in each athlete between victory and loss, whether it be a loss that helps the athlete learn or one that shatters the competitor and his self-image. Equally, we must know our athletes well enough to know where that balance point is in each of them.

Knowledge of the rules of the game. All too often competitors lose because they don't know every rule and how to apply it. And rules change. This is critical to remember. Constant "refresher courses" are a must even for the most knowledgeable coaches.

Teaching the Coach

One cannot teach what one does not know. This may sound obvious, but too many times coaches are assigned to sports in the public schools without the slightest knowledge of the game beyond what is written in the books and in the rulebook. The answer is clear: learn the sport, work at the sport, become proficient in the sport, and learn how to teach the sport. Just as a trained clarinet teacher cannot teach violin, a trained swimming coach cannot necessarily teach basketball. Each has a separate base of knowledge and skills.

Serious damage could be done by the well-meaning but ill-informed school coach who is assigned to teach out of his field. Again the answer is clear: make it your field. This means learn the sport or don't coach it. To me, however, one of the exciting things life has taught me is how much easier it is to learn a second sport once the first is mastered. This is true of any two compatible sports or a combination of multiple compatible sports. (I note compatible sports because there are sports where preparing for one interferes with the methods and skills of another.) This is why the triathlon and pentathlon have always been among my favorites. They allow one to expand, to build on current success. It also helps to break up some of the daily monotony of single sport drills.

Skills learned in one sport can many times add a new dimension to the attack or defense of another sport. Thus, the coach can bring new thinking to the competition on behalf of his athletes. This small margin of added knowledge can make the difference between victory and loss. There are very few sports competitions at the amateur level that result in what we call a "blow out." This is exactly why the NCAA has set up its divisions: to make the competition more equal. Thus, just a small edge in competitive knowledge and skill can make a big difference to the outcome.

The Power of Example

There are really only two ways to teach: by example and by precept. All other ideas fall into one of these two categories. *Example,* for its part, is the "do as I do" part of teaching. It presumes that the coach will live the role just as the student athletes expect. What is important is not just what expectation the coach has for himself, but also understanding what expectation the athletes have for him. When I see a coach who is seriously overweight, I think it must be very difficult for him to try to teach proper diet and conditioning to his athletes. I may not be as talented as some of my athletes, but they know I demand the best of myself as I demand the best of them.

Precept is teaching by principles. It is finding ways to help the athlete visualize correct methods, values, approaches, etc. And when combined with teaching by example, it can be a powerful tool for perfecting both the coach and the athletes.

A coach should never expect anything of his athletes that he himself is not prepared to do. Probably the greatest example of this in our century is the Israeli Army. It is legendary for its loyalty and its command excellence. It has survived against all odds. At no time has it been considered the underdog. But it has been led by a guiding principle: in Israel the military commanders lead from the front. They lose commanders, but not wars. In July of 1976, even as we in America were awakening to the celebration of our own nation's Bicentennial of Freedom, we learned of the daring rescue by Israeli commandos of hostages being held at the Entebbe Airport in Uganda. There was, as I recall, only one Israeli fatality in that mission so daringly executed and brilliantly conceived. It was the commander of the mission, a very young Israeli Colonel whose brother now serves with distinction as the Israeli Ambassador to the United Nations. Colonel Netanyatu's example of leadership will live forever in the annals of men and women fighting for freedom.

This same principle applies to coaching. A good coach takes care of his people first, himself last. He opens the door in the morning and closes it at night. Loyalty is not built on authority; it is an acceptance of the authority built on mutual respect. And respect is earned—not bestowed from on high. Once these basics are in place as a coach, the respect of the athletes for the coach is well on its way to fruition.

All of this combined begins to make a coach. It is only after this foundation has been laid that the coach can begin to do his "off the mat" work. I cannot overemphasize that these fundamentals must be in place or what is supposed to follow will not.

Chapter IX

Passing the Torch to America

GEORGE WASHINGTON could have been elected President for life. He was offered the title of King of the American Colonies, and declined it forcefully. But he believed that he—as an individual—was not important. He did not believe that he had a monopoly on wisdom, a superior understanding of world power or a vision toward which he was guiding the nation.

We, today, revere him for these qualities, and many more, but he himself did not. Rather, he saw himself as one man who sought to do the best he could with a new and divided group of colonies that had just declared itself a nation.

What he correctly understood was that it was more important to create a government that respected individual liberty, and with permanent institutions held by temporary occupants, than to take and hold power for himself. He did not see himself—or any other man—as indispensible. He did his duty, and then retired.

To him, this was what separated America from every other government in the world of his time. It was an entirely new basis of government, untried, but fervently believed to be correct.

Ours was to be a government of laws, not of men. Men were to come and go within the institutions, but never control them. The rights of the individual and individual economic interests were both respected in the new Constitution. Each was to give a little, and get a little. It was believed that the whole was, indeed, greater than the sum of the parts.

The Founding Fathers knew that humankind was fallible, but getting better. And President Washington wanted to ensure that each new generation (beginning with the one to follow him) would be given the opportunity to lead the nation before the previous one was too old to govern and too stubborn to give up.

And so, when his second term as President ended, he passed the torch on to a successor (from Massachusetts—not even Virginia) and retired to Mount Vernon. He never interfered with those who followed his footsteps into the Presidency.

He is honored and revered today, the Father of his country. And, like every good father, he allowed his children— the new, young leaders of this United States of America— first to crawl, then walk and finally run.

Imperfection Rules

We must remember that the nation we have inherited was never formed or nurtured in the belief that it (or any individual in it) was perfect. It was, quite literally, formed on the opposite premise: that we are all quite imperfect.

Therefore, the institutions of government which we created were to take all of our imperfections into account by making checks and balances a central theme. The three branches of government, the divisions of powers between the national and state governments, and between government and the people, all formed the system we know as federalism.

The purpose of this was rooted in the experience of having to deal with a king who was far less than perfect, and to ensure that one group could not arbitrarily impose its will on any other group. The same held true for individuals, even if they thought they had a "divine right" to govern.

All had to work together to form not a perfect union, but rather "a more perfect union." Implicit in this was the recognition that ours will never be a perfect union. The end, then, is to do the best to make it just a little better each generation.

These same values are with us today. In our society, we pass the torch to those who follow in the hopes that they will hold it higher than we did, and make it burn more brightly than our generation has. Like the torch that precedes each Olympic game, our values are passed from hand to hand until, hopefully, they will light the world.

Yet, unlike other "isms" of our time, we do not look forward to a withering away of the state, a thousand years of peace, or any other end. We just hope to make the world a little better than we received it, because we understand that we, too, make mistakes both as individuals and as a society.

Today we have a nation of fathers and mothers from every walk of life who daily pass the torch a little at a time to the next generation. Some of what we pass on is good, and some is disconcerting. For right alongside the rise in religious consciousness and a decline in cigarette smoking is the rise in cocaine use and teen suicide.

These values—both good and bad—are passed on in part by each of us, including coaches, athletic champions and just good competitors. By our example and what we are, we have the opportunity to pass on the values of sportsmanship, courtesy, courage, honor, grace, pride and endurance.

If we do, I have no doubt that the next generation will follow our example. If we do not, then we will have written our society's decline by our own lives. We will carve an epitaph on Freedom's headstone reading, "Early Death Due to Neglect."

A great nation is built on great and eternal values. Millions of its young see these values being lived by—and bringing joy to—the vast majority of its citizens. So, because of the example of those they wish to emulate, they follow. Young people seek role models of these virtues. When they find those qualities present in those they admire, they reach out for them and receive joy. When they find their "hero" lacks such values, they seek fulfillment elsewhere in friendless places where temporary pleasure replaces real joy.

It is these values that the torch must light. In the end it

doesn't really matter who wins on the field—what matters is what competition does for the individual competitors. For them it builds character.

But sports themselves are not a part of a war. In war there is a victor and a vanquished. Athletic competition is a game of skill and determination. It is a mechanism to build values of integrity, courage, moral conviction and self-respect rather than mere physical skills.

This is why the NCAA and its affiliated colleges are so concerned that college athletic departments carefully obey strict rules of individual and collegiate conduct. They know that the game is secondary to what really ought to be taught—off-the-mat values. And these are the same values that underlie a college education. It is teaching for life, both on and off the mat, in and out of the pool, but always in life and forever.

All too often we look to pass on wealth alone, as if it were an end and not a means. In my own case, I was fortunate to have received a sufficient inheritance. And I have been able to add to, increase and expand those resources. This is because I inherited much more than money. I inherited a strong sense of telling right from wrong, a strong sense of stewardship that demanded that these resources be used for a good beyond that of my mere support or luxury, and a responsibility to help this nation wherever I can. I help the kids because I want America to win.

That which endures is made of stronger stuff than money. It is the combined experiences of failure and success, of determination and heartbreak, that forge the iron ore of the young into the fine, tempered steel of the young adult. It determines whether the individual will be a giver or a taker in life.

Good Citizenship

The responsibility of good citizenship was taught early in our family. It came from the first du Pont in America, and was passed down to each generation. We were expected to understand what citizenship meant.

Three of the most important beliefs of good citizenship that we learned and have tried to practice are, first, a commitment to equality of opportunity, second, a firm belief in liberty, and third, a strong sense of justice.

Equality of Opportunity in America

Equality in America is a central value of our nation. Even if we fall short, we still hold it up as a direction we want our nation and its people to take. There is much evidence of this throughout cultural Americana, and it is well written into the folklore of our leaders and their examples.

We profess before the world that "all men are created equal" in the sight of God. Our nation was divided by a great Civil War because of this issue, and we hold those words and the ideals they embody even more sacred today than when Abraham Lincoln spoke them at Gettysburg more than one hundred years ago.

The struggle for equality rages everywhere in this world

today. Many nations currently are doing what we did over one hundred years ago—fighting for the principle of equality before God and their own government. We applaud that effort.

Additionally, we believe in "equal opportunity under the law." The changes in our system and in the hearts of our people in just the past thirty years in this area have been nothing short of miraculous. No one could have predicted the political and social changes in the Southern states or in the Northern cities.

Equally important it has been done with virtually no bloodshed even when the assassin's bullets horrified the nation in the middle 1960's. Instead, we have adjusted and moved forward into an era of the greatest equality yet known in this nation. And the pace continues.

Armed with an equal chance to succeed, the responsibility to be the role model lies with the gifted and talented of each generation. We depend on them to pass on the values leading to success in life. As they lead out, their actions and values will make the difference between success and failure for those who follow.

With Liberty

Liberty is the right of the individual to work out his own destiny, dream his own private dreams, and do so without the overbearing hand of his neighbors, the government or any other authority. More than any other principle, the

American Revolution was fought over this one idea: no one has the right to take away another person's "life, liberty or pursuit of happiness," not even a king.

Thomas Paine, Samuel Adams and Patrick Henry all became the eternal examples of this principle. As loyal followers of the law, it was difficult for them to break with their sovereign. But the immutable laws of liberty demanded independence. Their willingness to defy the reign of King George III—their King—tells us how important it was to them. It is still important today. As President Lincoln reminded us, our nation was "conceived in liberty." As I travel the world with my *Team Foxcatcher* athletes, I am ever more convinced of the righteousness of this cause for which our nation was born.

And Justice for All

Justice is the second value of citizenship. It is the application of the law fairly to all, for the benefits of all of society. It speaks to the needs of the whole, of the right of the nation to survive and prosper.

In war, for example, the needs of justice are strong. Even though individuals may not wish to serve in the armed forces, the right of the nation to survive as a whole is more important than the individual's right to protest. We are all expected to do our part in time of national crisis. In peace, the right of society to protect itself against disease, natural disaster and the human condition are equally important.

It is this principle that gives the people—through their duly elected leaders—the right (the right of eminent domain) to take, with just compensation paid to the owners, privately owned property for the purpose of creating a larger public good, such as a road, a school, a dam or whatever.

We are all Americans, whether we choose to lead a public or a private life, and whether we choose to participate with others or choose to live alone. Ours is a heritage of responsibility. If we shirk this very public obligation then we have nothing to pass on, and therefore, we have made a useful life meaningless.

On Citizenship

There is nothing new about citizenship. It is as ancient as civilization. So is the history of failed civilizations that have not taught their young the basic values that have made civilizations great. It is our belief that equality, liberty and justice are three of the most important attributes of a great nation if that nation is to endure.

We have the same responsibility as leaders of other previous civilizations. We coaches. We trainers. We athletes. We parents. We peers. WE THE PEOPLE.

Our values do not emanate from the President down. They start with the people and move up. After all, we choose our leaders from among us, rather than *vice versa*.

Again, it is not wealth. We have been blessed with more

wealth than any nation on the face of the earth in history. But if we—the richest nation on earth—lose our sense of spiritual direction and guiding values, then no amount of wealth will regain our place in the world, or our opportunity to do good on God's earth.

Our greatness comes from much more than our status as the richest nation on earth. Our achievements are too many to number:

- We began our nation with the widest voting franchise on earth. We have extended the free right to vote to all adults in America. All are franchised.

- The laws are created to protect everyone equally no matter how unpopular their cause or how private their desires.

- No nation has ever been more generous in granting citizenship to the homeless, the deprived or the poor. Ours is a country of immigrants who have built a nation.

- When faced with the challenge of space, America safely placed the first man on the moon. And it has shared its knowledge and resources with other nations for their benefit.

- The United States of America is the world's "bread-basket." We feed the world's starving, clothe the naked everywhere, and support freedom fighters around the globe.

- We have always extended the hand of friendship to our conquered enemies. After World War II the Marshall Plan and reconstruction of Japan were unprecedented acts of generosity and compassion.

These and all other liberties we now enjoy need to be taught and lived by all who profess to be true Americans. Citizen athletes, like every other high achiever group in our nation, need to understand this broader picture of what they can achieve by example and by precept. They need to be aware that others see in them what they themselves would like to become.

We Americans face not a rendezvous with destiny so much as a crusade for liberty. WE THE PEOPLE, each of us, as individuals and as a people are both the legatees and the guarantors of our current and future freedoms. We seek not just the individual liberty of one, but the indivisible liberty of all. We are our own best hope and security for America's future and the world's freedom. Ours is the initiative to seize and the victory to win. When that day comes, we will unlock the higher fraction of the human spirit, and then we will all be citizens of a new generation, one that is destined to fulfill and to live out the promise of the American Dream for all.

The Beginning